# Also by Robert Pinsky

POETRY

NONFICTION

# Proverbs of Limbo

FARRAR STRAUS GIROUX / NEW YORK

# Robert Pinsky

# Proverbs of Limbo

## Poems

Farrar, Straus and Giroux

120 Broadway, New York 10271

Printed in the United States of America

First edition, 2024

Library of Congress Cataloging-in-Publication Data

Names: Pinsky, Robert, author.

Title: Proverbs of limbo : poems / Robert Pinsky.

Description: First edition. | New York : Farrar, Straus and Giroux, 2024.

Identifiers: LCCN 2023051858 | ISBN 9780374611958 (hardcover)

Subjects: LCGFT: Poetry.

Classification: LCC PS3566.I54 P76 2024 | DDC 811/.54—dc23/eng/20231117

LC record available at https://lccn.loc.gov/2023051858

Designed by Crisis

Our books may be purchased in bulk for promotional, educational,
or business use. Please contact your local bookseller or the Macmillan
Corporate and Premium Sales Department at 1-800-221-7945, extension
5442, or by email at MacmillanSpecialMarkets@macmillan.com.

www.fsgbooks.com

Follow us on social media at @fsgbooks

10 9 8 7 6 5 4 3 2 1

To L.G.

# Contents

# Proverbs
# of
# Limbo

# Poem of Names

The bad rain fell on Osamu Shimomura.
On the walk home it turned his white shirt black.
"My grandmother got me quickly into a bath.
It likely saved me from death by radiation."

Tougaloo's Ernst Borinski would not discuss
His family, killed by Nazis: "An area I
Have liquidated, for my mental health."
His grave at Tougaloo a kind of shrine.
Salma begat Boaz and Boaz begat Obed:
Underground river of passion and retrenchment.

Thank you, Elliot, Simon & Hazel, for wanting
To talk with me about my dying some day—
Bucky had been so cold when you touched his body.
A compliment for me, that conversation.
It almost doesn't matter what we said.
I thought of Milford your great-grandpa, that time
I asked him, did he believe in life after death?
"I guess that you are my life after death," he said.

A boy named Christian, at a Q & A in Texas,
Asked me, the visiting poet, "What motivates you—
What gets you out of bed each day?" Good question.
The pride of Ernst Borinski, of Mississippi.
The shame of Nathan Forrest, of Pillow Hill.
Willie Lee Rose, Historian of Reconstruction.
Congressman Pellegrino Rodino, called Pete.

It's the dead people that motivate me, Christian.
Dorothy Pinsky Wright. William Butler Yeats.
As to your name, I remember Don Polk saying
"A lot of Jewish people think they're white.
But, no they're not." In some ways Yeats was a jerk.
Arphaxad begat Salah. Salah begat Eber.
"Oh yeah?" said Ruby to Don. "Well, most Black people
Don't know they're goyim."

                                    Somebody said about
Rodino and Sirica, "The night-school guys
Are saving the country." Borinski needed a job
But no white school could offer him a position—
Tougaloo did. At his famous Forums there,
He asked his students to sit one chair apart
So the white kids from Millsaps sat among them.
Pete Seeger, Ralph Bunche, Joan Baez at the Forums.
Rodino in the House impeaching Nixon.

*Pellegrino* means pilgrim.

Shimomura

Discovered cells that made a jellyfish glow.

He garnered a million samples in Puget Sound.

A protein in *Aequorea victoria*, embedded

To glimmer in other life, transformed the study

Of living things. Years later, the Exxon *Valdez*

Oil spill left nearly all those *Aequorea* dead,

A poisoning that Shimomura indicted—

He whose grandma had washed away the ashes.

# Branca

Ralph Branca was the fifteenth of seventeen children.
This poem is not the poem of "the speaker."

His father was an immigrant from Calabria.
These words are those of Robert Pinsky. Speaking.

Branca wore Dodger uniform number 13.
"Speaking" is the punch line of a Jewish joke.

Some Romans call Calabrians "Africani."
Brooklyn had its own daily, the *Brooklyn Eagle*.

At eighty-five Branca learned about his mother.
He was twenty-one when Robinson joined the Dodgers.

At eleven I loved Robinson for his daring
Running the bases. Stealing home. His fire.

Branca was one of the few who befriended him.
I was too young to understand his mission

The fuel of that dancing to taunt the pitcher.
Robinson never forgot Branca's kindness.

What the old man found out about his mother
Is she was born a Jew in Hungary. Kati.

After he gave up the most famous home run ever,
Back in the clubhouse Branca lay weeping face down.

Kati gave birth to seventeen Catholic children.
The Giants won the pennant. 1951.

Branca means "claw," a fit name for a pitcher.
His teammates thought it best that he cry alone,

But "Only my dear friend Jackie, who knew me so well,
Came over and put his arm around my shoulder."

The Nazis killed the aunts and uncles Branca
Didn't know existed until he was old.

42 in itself a nothing of a number.
The Dodgers traded Branca to the Tigers.

Grief: with its countless different ways and strains.
Glory: a greater thing than success, but slower.

Some of the Tigers who had been Giants explained
To Branca how the Giants had stolen the signs

From opposition catchers. The telescope
In center field. Wires, buzzers. Branca chose not

To talk about it. It's all in Prager's book.
His research unearthed Kati, those aunts and uncles.

The Dodgers were taken from Brooklyn by their owner:
I, Robert Pinsky, choose not to say his name.

I didn't live in Brooklyn but I knew the score.
I knew it was a kind of underdog place.

Nowadays once a year all Major Leaguers
Wear Jackie Robinson's number 42.

In the joke, the person who answers the telephone
At Goldberg, Goldberg and Goldberg keeps replying

That Goldberg is out of the office. And so is Goldberg.
"Alright, then let me talk to Goldberg." "Speaking."

Robinson spoke to Branca: "Without you"
He said, "We never could have made it this far."

# At Mt. Auburn Cemetery

Walking among the graves for exercise
Where do you get your ideas how do I stop them
Looking for Mike Mazur's marker I looked
Down at the grass and saw Stanisław Barańczak
Our Solidarity poetry reading in Poznań
Years later in Newton now he said I'm a U.S.
Liberal with a car like everybody else
When I held Bobo dying in my arms
His green eyes told me *I am not done yet*
Then he was gone when he was young he enjoyed
Leaping up onto the copy machine to press
A button and hear it hum to life and rustle
A blank page then another out onto its tray
Sometimes he batted the pages down to the floor
I used to call it his hobby here's a marble
Wicker bassinet marking a baby's grave
To sever the good fellowship of dust the vet's
Needle first a sedative then death now Willie
Paces the house mowling his elegy for Bobo
They never meow to one another just to people
Or to their nursing mother when they're small I

Marvel at this massive labeled American elm
Spreading above a cluster of newer names
Chang, Ohanessian, Kondakis joining Howells,
Emerson, Shaw and here's a six-foot sphere
Of polished granite perfect and inscribed WALKER
Should I have let him die his own cat way
The cemetery official confided Bruce Lee
Spends less on a stone than Schwarzenegger what
Will mark the markers when like mourners they bow
And kneel and fall down flat to kiss the heaps
They have in trust under the splendid elm
Also marked with its tag a noble survivor
Civilization lifted my cat from the street
Gave him a name his shots and managed his death
Now Willie howls the loss from room to room
When people say I'm ashamed of being German
Said Arendt I want to say I'm ashamed of being
Human sometimes when Bobo made his copies
Of nothing I'd crumple one for him to chase
And combat in the game of being himself.

# The Funnies, 1949

I liked not knowing why Major Hoople wore a fez: more
Pleasure in just knowing there was a kind of thing to know.

It was like not having the means to know Fifth Avenue,
Pico Boulevard, The Loop, Piccadilly any ordinary way,

Unsure which street might be in which city—a lordly joy,
To dream up the place a story's detective was telling.

Hoople was a blowhard and a faker, not really a major. Some
Might call his fez an orientalist token of affected high-class ease.

But the same way *Prince Valiant* and *Smilin' Jack* were partly
About knighthood and airplanes they were also all the better

If you had a spark of Hoople in you, to detect mysteries more
Telling than they looked, for a child to wonder at: intimations

In how the women were drawn. Or in the two kinds of foreigner:
Evil or funny—and was I one?—in "the poor man's encyclopedia."

# Forgiveness

The mind skitters, its one rudder
Being its own voice. The great
Fascist poet taught me free verse.

Trying to concentrate on "The forgiving
Of an unforgivable crime" in a lecture
By Emmanuel Levinas, I drift into
Keely Smith being Cherokee.

"The desire for *vers libre*," says Pound
In his hectoring way, is "quantity
Reasserting itself after years
Of starvation." Reading that, I
Got the idea—just like in music,
Longer is different from higher.

Like with long "ee"s,
And it was called "quantity"—
I could hear it. The third syllable
Longer, the first one stressed by pitch:
Bitterness. Cherokee. Popinjay.

I don't pretend I was thinking
About the Trail of Tears or any other
Unforgivable crime. I was thinking
About how well she imitates
Louis Prima's pelvis-forward walk, mocking
The magic of it while singing like
An angel in a prom dress, and how
Great it would be to write something
That funny and impassioned.

The cadences and quantities
Of his "Exile's Letter" break my heart
As a ritual of truth, the remote
Spoken ceremony of atonement.

At the same time, I scorn
That nostalgic celebration of drunken
Friendship among exquisite
Diplomats of an ancient ruling class.
Starvation a figure of speech!

The airy dynamo of song
Animates the shadows.

And speaking of shadows, who has
A right to forgive? White soldiers

Took away the Arapahos' horses.
In old Ukraine, the Nationalists first
Mutilated some Jews, then made them
Dance and sing naked before
Killing them, as a way of showing
What they'd like to do to the Poles,
Or was it the invading Germans. Is the point
Humiliation beyond forgiveness?

Do the damned impregnate
The enslaved to make an
Unforgivable point? Also to deny it?
Even poor John Keats, in his letters,
Enjoys a little minor Jew baiting.
Who do I think I am to forgive him?
After all, I am him. He too was the child
Of a New Jersey optician and please do me
A favor, don't tell me No he wasn't.

# Soul Making

Galactic broth visible light-years away
Brews the first suns. Familial, I feel
I know these lights. I see their pre-biotic
Geometries of purpose the way I impose

Human, nearly literary intentions
Onto the microscopic animals, flexing
Bizarre mandibles, that patrol my eyelids
And guts. Brothers and sisters electronically

Revealed, arcane mute dynasties of being:
Darkling I too perform the turns and bits
Of my assigned proportions. Feigning
Rapt comprehension, I know you the way

An infant pretends amazement each time
The mother with a spoon tip searching
Under the jar's rim finds more and yet
More of the strained *Apricots and Apples*:

Infant, the sunflower turns toward her, deep
Egypt of shared attachment and concealment,
Tangy preserved sweetness forging in turn
The courtly generation of—call it a soul.

# Place Name Echoes

*In memory of Adam Zagajewski*

As a child's idea of blood is a scraped knee, I heard them
As New Jersey names: old Mr. Lyman the shamus
Crooning the prayers under his breath all day long.
Mr. Chernovitz. Manny and Bea Mirapol.

Hidden in the homely consonants, echoes of blood.
Jerry Lewis changed from Levitch, Ukrainian for Levi.
In the shul Yossel Tarnapol a Survivor, always smiling
In his bad clothes. Murder again exploding in Babin Yar

That is to Babi Yar as Kyiv is to Kiev, chasms of blood
In one spelled shade of pronunciation or another,
The Lvov of Adam's poem is Lviv. Mr. Lemberg from
Vilnius Wilno Vilna—instrument of cousin tongues,

And every tongue a fanged familiar spirit. To expel
In air the blood-stunned music of time, a spoken
Makeshift calm or explosion. Fate saturates names.
Death awaits you, he wrote, calling the city by name

In the name of the Earth. In all degrees of translation
Every city a Jerusalem, every person a Jew, a city
Contorted exhales the syllables of its name, plain
As a peach, over again in each chorus of its blood.

# Vocal

Infinite information here in my phone.
Here in my head a congregation of dead
With numbers I had by heart, each with a tune
Back when a few years' friendship in New Brunswick
Or Palo Alto was a lifetime. The numbers
Now fast asleep among the neuron ruins.

Thwarted by the Elders he defied, Gene England
A hero now for those young Mormons I met.
Henry Dumas shot dead by a transit cop.
He told me once while we were reading "The Gyres"
That as an airman in Texas he could get in
To see movies with an accent and a turban.

To keep a number you might first write it down
Then teach your fingers a little samba of clicks,
The jagged keypad steps in a tactile rhythm
Set by a chant of practical voodoo. Vocal:
As intimate as a given name. The spell,
*Seven-oh-one, Eight-six Two-two*, remembered.

# Country Music

Ifeanyi says in his country a baby
Is *It* until it learns to be one of *Us*.

I am in my Igbo second childhood.
The coral, a quarrel, a glacier, my lungs.

The weather, the world, the book review.
Lyrical bitching. Biblical plaint. Infant

Debt of attention vetting the news,
The noise, the needs, for keeps. It is

The world's beginnings, my own endings,
And having the heart to tell them apart.

# Revisionary

The globe on a tilted axis means The News.
As the icon spins the angle seems to shift.

Science has found ancestral Neanderthals.
We have a bit of their blood. They painted caves
Better than *sapiens*, as we named ourselves.

History has found the Jews who fought for Hitler.
Thousands of Part and what were called Full Jews.
A few were generals.
                                    As the globe revolves
Different mixes keep passing into the light
Or into the dark, and then back out again:

Over and over again, the unexpected.

Jefferson's July 2 draft blamed George III
For violating the liberty of a "People
Who never offended him" shipped off to be
"Slaves in another hemisphere." For many
"Miserable death in transportation thither."
On July 4, that passage was left out. Thither.

In draft after draft of *Pudd'nhead Wilson* Twain
Linked and tore apart stories: Conjoined twins
From Italy charm a town. In that same town, two
Blue-eyed babies. The nursemaid fair-skinned Roxy
Secretly swaps the babies cradle to cradle,
Different nightie to nightie and race to race.
The one is her son. He will sell her down the river.

# Cataract

It doesn't fall it gathers the doctor explained:
That's just what people named it. When I took off
The bandage I was blinded by glare—not shielded
Now by the clouded lenses I was born with.
The clear new rigid plastic let in the full
Untempered brightness falling from the air.
*Niagara*. Film noir betrayals. None can well
Behold with eyes what underneath him lies,
Colors of betrayal as clear as black and white
In the pines, the pines, where the sun never shines.
The fog that falls as tree-drip feeds the Sequoias.
Yosemite they say means "killers" in Miwok:
Word one group called another. The European
Militias in the Gold Rush killed all the groups.
In Berkeley, Ishi was called the Last of His People.
It wasn't one people, he was a mix, it wasn't
His name he explained, clearly he had no name
With no one to call him by a name. Bob says
The way that poetry works is John Muir took
Theodore Roosevelt to see the Falls. Wonder

Begotten by eyes. Muir inspired by Thoreau,
Thoreau read Wordsworth—so, the national parks.
Gail remembers Maisie LeBlanc and Nina
DeSantis pulling down her pants to see
Did Jews have tails. Ishi the last of more than
One people. In Ha Jin's book a singer in exile,
His song of grief for the mother his native country
Forbade him to visit. Somebody in an essay
Called it a song of love for the Motherland,
Punishing the singer with bad poetry. Loss
Too gathers and also falls. My eyes adjusted
So I could name the people and things I saw,
Murmurous comfort like chanted begats of descent,
Each name a shadow's elegy and a presence.
The great portcullis of years, descending. "Ishi"
Means fellow, a person. The trailer promoting *Niagara*
Called it a raging torrent of blind emotion.

# Nature Study

Does the bird hop or walk? And when it lands
Does it lean back and spread its wings to slow
Or does it dive head first and swoop? The veins
Of the leaf: do they radiate from a center
Like fingers from a hand? Or do they branch
Out from a line like tree limbs from a trunk?

The stomach of consciousness needs to fill itself,
As when the sea star embraces a clam or mussel.
The pentacle of suckers pulls for an hour
To create a hairline cleft, then the star vomits
Its own insides, and then the intelligent stomach
Oozes blind and purposeful into the host.

# Geronimo

They say paratroopers still yell *Geronimo* when they jump
Because of a movie the first ones saw, the one with Geronimo

Played by Chief Thundercloud, the first Tonto, real name
Victor Daniels, not the one with him played by Chuck Connors

Who played for the Dodgers and later played the Rifleman,
Which became a nickname of Flemmi a mob killer in Boston.

In real life he came home to find soldiers had killed his mother
His young wife and his children. That's not in the movie.

Somewhere sometime someone must have yelled *Geronimo* as
Syllables to voice when they were about to commit an atrocity.

They told me Germans murdered our cousins, so I was mean
To Leander. His German parents were Nana's tenants.

Good pitching beats good hitting, and vice versa—I never
Said half of what I said. Bless Yogi Berra leaving it knotted

Like all things that are more than one thing, and all people
For our unwitting and witting witless improvised mixtures.

Bless all the knots never known to be true or not true for
Showing me my impurity in proportions unknowable and vital.

Bless Nana my grandmother for her Southern accent in English
And her Romanian accent in Yiddish, that I echo still unwitting

As with respectful misquotations and innocent mistakes that
Sometimes correct the authorities. His name was not Geronimo.

I was not a chief he said, never was a chief, but because I was
More deeply wronged than others the title was conferred on me.

Berra in Hebrew means a good person, in Arabic a truth-teller.
Or is it a town in Ferrara, or a hut dweller, or Spanish *berrear*?

In a gym Larry with a towel on his head or sitting some way
They said looked like a Yogi—these things fit or stick. Leander's

Torn sneakers showed foot skin that I stomped, like one of the jerks
Harvey Korman's character assembles in *Blazing Saddles*.

Let them go, says Brooks in warpaint on horseback in Yiddish.
Jay Silverheels played Tonto the most, an actual Mohawk who

Got to say the punch line: They fired me when they found out what
"Kemosabe" means. The joke may be obsolete, but for me it plays

In the sacred field of the unknown, with meanings abounding.
The title was conferred on me, he said, and I resolved to honor it.

# Beatitudes

The sting ray flies, the penguin swims
And the nightshade harms and heals
Like the spear of a hero.

Protect the silkworm, and the bear who
Created the world, from Mammon
As Allen Ginsberg forewarned.

Thank god for boredom, the great
Eventual deflator of all fads
And spurious elevations,

For without it we would be suffocated
By centuries of baloney,
And have nothing.

There are Jews of Asia descended from
Sephardic and Ashkenazi traders
Of silk and spices.

Over centuries away from Wilno or Morocco
Their rituals evolved. Their faces resemble
Those of their neighbors.

Spica, one of the brightest stars in our sky,
Is a rotating ellipsoidal variable in
Celestial terms of meaning.

Bless even "To facilitate understanding and to work
With creative aspects of our process as
Innovative means of transformation,"

For behold how those other words accumulate
Their syllable-clatter to make *Work*
Shine like a lost sapphire.

August laughed when for the anime
Name I couldn't pronounce I
Substituted Moskowitz.

Spica was also the Shepherd mix of the Hansons,
Who named her for the initials of
Her birthplace the SPCA.

Mr. Hanson wore a yarmulke at my Bar Mitzvah
And so too did Joe Purcell
And Woodie Alessi.

Bless the horse chestnut for the humility
Of the inedible, and bless the phrases
"Horse pill" and "horse comb"

That recognize the nature of the nearly
Useless and the cumbersome,
For after all who isn't?

Praise my mother saying "schtick pfaerd,"
To call someone a part of a horse
While not specifying the part,

Which makes it both more courteous
And funnier, in the way of Yiddish
And Emily Dickinson.

On the High Holy Days, we kids gambled
With horse chestnuts, closest one
To the shul wall wins. Bless

My lumpy shooter chestnut for not rolling
When I tossed it, showing a jagged
Bounce too has its virtues.

# Not Minding

Wild parrots in a storm on Russian Hill
Screech their one vowel and eat the cherry blossoms,
Not minding the February rain and wind.

Buddhism here in the Bay is fresh and cool.
In Seoul it seemed aloof or feudal. The abbot
With his corona of monks, none of my business.

Many of the new Koreans now are Christians.
The teaching says: If you are feeling depressed,
Likely you need to think about death more often.

I concentrate, back straight, on each slow breath
With one same word imagined preceding speech
To approach the mystery of speech in silence.

# At the Paramount

My heart is a streak of cloud
Across a moon that
Shatters in the lake it lights.

It is also this palace with
Its pilasters and sconces
Pulsing to old music.

An urban dandelion fractures
The courtyard fore-lobby
Pavers trod by descendants

Of enslaved Africans
And peasants from Grodno
To Taiwan with telltale

Names like the blacklisted
Sympathizers haunting
Balcony and loge.

Muffled by its curtain
The infinite blank screen
Glitters and mumbles.

# In Barcelona

Are you Italian? Ignacio asked me. Thank you
I said in Spanish, I am a Jew of New Jersey.
And I, a Jew of Venezuela, he answered.

As Ellen said, If he was improvising
So much the better. The art of conversation:
Projecting in turns onto the screen of being.

# La Cucaracha

*The cockroach ah the cockroach he cannot travel*
*Because he lacks, because he does not have,*
*Marijuana to smoke.* I thought the Spanish
Felt more polite than English. I thought I read
An essay by Ramiro de Maeztu, saying
Hamlet and Don Quixote, born the same year
Were twins of action and inaction: Stop thinking—
Do something, the English audience pleads to Hamlet.
Don't do so much, for God's sake *think*, the Spanish
Reader implores Quixote. But I disliked
"National Character." I disliked God
For reasons that included forbidding pork.
A better example, the tower of Babel, punished
With Aramaic, English, Russian, Spanish.

*Please kindly come with me, I will marry you,*
*A spotted cockroach says to a little black one—*
Like the boll weevil "just lookin' for a home."

I didn't understand Maeztu was merely
Discussing an essay written by Turgenev.

God maybe was protecting the rainforest of
Multiple tongues against our monolith Babel.

In multiple ways I lacked, I did not have,
So much I ought to know, the Spanish subjunctive
Being the least of it. The spotted cockroach
Like Hamlet talks *viajar y casar* but never
Arrives or marries. Does the weevil find a home?
Quixote dithers too: like his Danish sibling
A devotee of language. In the Civil War,
Maeztu died taking the Fascist side. I forgive
The preacher for thorny sayings like, The poor you'll
Always have with you, as a way of asking:
What do you know, who do you think you are?—
Always too willing to judge, or not willing enough.

# Lenny Bruce

I saw him in San Francisco at the Purple Onion
When I was still at Stanford, a Teaching Assistant
Getting the "Ode to a Nightingale" by heart.

Out of prison on bail, soon he would die.
One of the charges against him was saying "shmuck."
He reminded me of my teacher Irving Howe:

The impatience of an improvising spirit
Hurtling beyond a footnote or a punch line
Like a light-wingèd dryad in the trees.

The comic with months to live was only 40.
I thought he talked too much about his trials—
Forgive me please, I was barely 24.

The cover charge, on my tiny fellowship,
A tender gesture menaced by hornets and grackles.
"Is money all you people think about?"

Being a lizard I'm not sure what to say.
John Keats in a letter says that now he's ready
"To cheat as well as any literary Jew"—

One more example, ho hum, how could it matter
To me as a secret reptile from outer space
Charmed by your human poetry and music?

Howe happened to be at Stanford that one year.
My poetry teacher Yvor Winters deplored
The "awful mess" of Keats's mind. I did

Get him to concede the "Ode" was beautiful.
He seemed surprised and happy when I told him
Howe had assigned his essay on Henry James.

"Alright, it's true! We killed him. What a bad scene,
It was us, my family did it, we found a note *I
Killed Jesus* in the basement, signed Cousin Morty."

I'm grateful to Lenny Bruce for saying that.
I pardon Keats for being a shmuck—the word
A homey metaphor meaning a bangle, a gem,

Diminutive for a child is shmeckel, a spoken
Precious ornament weighed and appreciated
In the jazzy sacred scales of appropriation.

# Beach Glass

Who knew this too could become endangered or extinct?
They gave me a little pail so I collected beach glass and shells.
Who knew the sound in a seashell wasn't your own blood—
No more than the ocean? It was the shell's chambers breathing,

A voice of air: Not churning breakers, nor a pulse in your ear.
In the sun's furnace glare, the smooth cloudy gemstones
Couched an interior fire. Like shells, progeny of the beach.
Who knew the soothing talcum could engender fatal tumors?

Cobalt from Phillips' Milk of Magnesia. Emerald from Coke.
Vitalis, My Sin, Serutan—the restless brine of years
Dusted their mute glitter. I had a friend once who loved
Buying the water that came sealed in plastic: Nature visibly

Mastered by invention. Who knew that perfect clarity could
Throttle the ocean itself? Did the chemicals make him sick?
Prone on the sand, I studied an inch from my eye the jagged
Clear granules they told me were seeds of molten glass.

# Being a Ghost

When they die I become a ghost
Afloat from room to room as vague
In grief as when I can't find my keys.

Some say zombies became popular
When our phones got so smart we began
To stagger staring at them, entranced.

Alone without my dead to phone
I'm left adrift as when I can't
Remember a name I know I know,

Darkward appalled ghost-mind aghast
At the crowd of names all stranded alive
Ashore, outwaiting my shadowy boat.

# Cosmopolitan Confessions

Taking her stand against God and government
She bought her eight-year-old a BLT
On toast at Woolworth's counter, for all to see—
So I could become a sophisticated person,

She told me. Maybe she wanted me to know
That the great ordinary gentile world
Could offer something better than Blood and Soil.
She was ten years older than Allen Ginsberg
Of Newark, author of *Cosmopolitan Greetings*.
Defy the holy. Notice what you notice.

Gauge the norms of provinces and metropoles:
"Cosmopolitan" for a magazine, a drink.
Could Sylvia know the word as Allen did,
A scholarly slur for a rootless Jewy Jew?

The sandwich was heaven. But in her kosher house
The unclean take-out pizza had to be eaten
From off the piano bench, with paper plates.
She wouldn't touch it even if it was veggie.

Like Whitman she knew to contradict herself.
She savored consonants and spoke the worldly
Vowels of truth. Her brother Julie was in
The Battle of the Bulge the one same night
She and their mother separately saw him appear
Ghostlike and asking for coffee. In their kitchens
A mile apart the bonded enemies, mother
And daughter, both woke to brew that soldier a cup,
Which maybe let him survive. The universe,
Shapely and subjective. Mussolini died
In a newsreel. Hitler vanished. A sentient pig
Should not have died for my illumination,
And yet I thank my mother and I taste it again.

# What Kind of Name Is That

Nice people like us will rank the one same folder
Differently if the name is "Michael Carruthers"
Than if we're told it comes from "Tashawna Johnson,"

Tilted by syllables in what the experts call
Unconscious bias, betraying how much more
We learn to swallow than we ever know.

Cannibalism for the Brazilian poets
And painters who founded *Anthro-po-pha-gismo*,
Meant that their culture could devour the past:

To take a mouthful of Portuguese and chew,
To excrete the husk and transmutate the pith
Into new kinds of muscle and bone and nerve.

Returned and taking a walk in his dear New York,
Henry James likens the Jews he hears to snakes
Or big-nosed fish swarming the Lower East Side,

The all-unconscious impudence of those mouths
The agency of the future ravage of English.
*What kind of name is that?*—to some the question

Sounds innocent: *with an* i *or with a* y*?*
To tune the ear for that familiar music:
Armenian suffix, Italian terminal vowels.

The *anthropophagismos* had in mind
Pedro Sardinha, authoritarian Bishop
Eaten by oppressed Caeté in 1556.

The name Sardinha might be demeaned in Boston.
You dirty Portugeezer, they yelled at Mario:
Possibly so, he said, why bring it up?

A carful guessed the wrong slur for Mohit,
An amused Hindu from Georgia they thought Hispanic.
Why do we call them "slurs"? My doctor recalls

A Yankee professor who assured his class
Tashawna feels pain less than Michael. *Yankee*
Maybe first meant a *Jankel*, a name the English

Could call a New York Dutchman. Henry James,
Grieving for how his native city and language
Were passing away into a limbo monstrous

Beyond imagination, passed the tenement
Where in a cramped apartment the infant brothers
Yakov and Ira Gershowitz lived, their name

Americanized to Gershwein. Yakov evolved
To Yankel, then *anthro-po-pha-gismoed* to George:
Namesake of kings and a dragon-killing saint.

# Privacy

In the World War some say has never ended
A Pole waited for his train. The cold of Hell.
The overcrowded Terminal stank and rumbled.
Each week a new law to amuse the public.
("Jews are no longer permitted to own a cat.")

On the marble stairs, a colony of beggars.
Overhead speakers roaring propaganda.
What was the word, he wondered, for what he saw:
A peasant family, their cloth spread on the floor
With mismatched floral crockery. Bread and tea,

Syntax of gestures, handing a child a cup.
They likely were illiterate he thinks,
Still wondering as an old man in America.
Once teaching a slave to read was against the law
Yet sometimes, more or less covertly, it happened.

Are online Forms a form of overcrowding?
Some of us click the box DECLINES TO ANSWER.

Thinking in his mother tongue he recalls the loaf
They carved, that formal alphabet of custom
Public in the soiled Station but somehow, private.

# Obituary

The only page that's always all about life,
Latin for "gone down," *pues* cooler than "grief."

The other pages of News are all about death.
*Nu* what went down, what's up or underneath?

"*Nu*, so what's new?" the ironic *bubbe* says
Like Cardenal who writes in Somoza's voice:

I know you people will tear my statue down.
It's not memorial. It's there to give you pain.

*Pues* the obits. All described and ranked.
*Nu*, homo sapiens, by our own works extinct.

All: *Populi*, tyrants, jerks, protectors. Children:
Weep for their *philo-sophia*. To know, see, listen.

Our deathless computers will browse these idle files—
*Pues*, our records. *Nu*, more just than our wills.

In Spanish and Yiddish, a word the sound of waiting
For what may be worth saying, which may be nothing.

# Adagio

More than midway along the feeling changes.
The adagio traffic plunges, or maybe it rises

From dolent meditation to vibrato chanting.
*Want-want* and again, a punctuated longing.

After the stroke or the loss or the deafness or after
The bad election, the movement's harsher or sweeter.

One day the music emerges a little distorted
From the thwarted mouth *un poco deformato*

And yet if it doesn't seem a moment's thwart
Our *pizzicato* stitching and stretching fall short,

*Ah ma non troppo.* In time the lines returned:
A reprieve, a refrain, an altered chord sustained.

*Want-want* the cello mourns and the waters rise
And fall on the stars and break in years and days.

# Repetition

Writer blighter fighter what do you want?
To repeat myself as does my fumbling heart,
*Thud-thud*—the microbe clangor of every cell
Rehearsing all of evolution, the mind
Enacting again anew a clash of doctrines.

I want to publish a book with on every page
The one same poem, all not by me but mine.
The Lamentation of the Fiery Furnace or
Tales of the Passage the Chorus of the Many
The Celebration of Ancestors Not by Blood,
*Thud-thud*, the Few the Many the One the Other.

The mixed chorus on every page struggles
To repeat again the birthright I cannot claim
Without accepting the inheritance again.
The Chorus of the Money the Execration
Of Light the Woman Who Deceived the Nazis.
Mixed voices on the cover. And at the end

The prophecy says to turn your back on the shore,
And lug your battered oar far inland, until
You find a people who don't know what the quaint
Artifact might be, although they do admire it
As a relic of that ancient rumour, the ocean—
The chorus of all us dead and all we want.

# Leo Gorcey

The same name as the famous actor I
Am one of the last people to remember.
It's possible the two of them were cousins.

I called him Uncle Leo. That was the custom
Among that generation on the margins:
Young in America, improvising cousins.

Soon the computer itself will tell these stories.
He was a plumber. My mother said his fingers
Had oil-burner soot ingrained under the skin.

He was their Eighth Grade Valedictorian.
I wonder if the name goes back to Gorczyn,
A town in Poland a few miles west of Łódz.

Public school was supposed to fill a void
Between democracy and capitalism.
Shakespeare and algebra and enough to eat.

The computer says I need to mention the Uncle
Leo in *Seinfeld*, but that's not who I mean.
Maybe I live in the fifties more than the nineties.

My father had a uniform for *Gorcey's Oilers*,
A basketball team that Uncle Leo sponsored.
Like boxing it used to be a Jewish game.

His father was the Gorcey plumber before him.
Everyone blamed him for making Leo quit school
But the old plumber wanted his son for a partner.

Maybe today a smart kid might quit school
To teach my computer how to write my poem.
Was "ingrained soot" a parable? What could it mean?

Small like his parents, who were Jewish and Irish,
The actor played a lowclass Dead End Kid
Named Muggs or Jock in a gang in a dozen movies.

My Uncle Leo was tall. His skin was clean.
The computer tells me there's a Gorcey's Plumbing
Still at the same address. It shows me the map.

# The Rag Trade

And what do you think the owners did with the cotton?
In Manchester and in Boston, a Golden Age
For nineteenth century mills. Desire still spins

Five dollar T-shirts, five hundred dollar jeans.
Rag trade cheap labor makes the world go around.
My grandpa was a rag picker. Who was yours?—

The Fords and Rockefellers in their Foundations
Looked for solutions to man-forged social ills
In means, markets and goods. A newer non-profit

Is after a cure for death. In blurred video
The cop yells, "Get the baby girl out of there."
The jury found him innocent: he killed while scared.

The mother tells him, "*Sir, you shot my boyfriend.*"
Foundations are driven by fashion and by desire.
One asked me, "Is this an educational project,

Or is it a project of public art?" I spring
From retail, what I felt like saying was,
Which is the answer where you give me money?

# Talking

It can be a way of thinking. There are people
Who fear it more than flying or heights or dying.
To be all talk is being less than nothing but
"Now you're talking" is more than you were before.

"I like how when he takes me to the market
He talks to all the packages," Debbie said,
Not long before she died. "He talks to lettuce."

I'm talking to you now. I talk to the cat.

In the frozen queue of grief at Stalin's prison
The question to Akhmatova: Can you
Describe this? "Yes," the poet answers, "I can."

The child's hand on her throat can feel her voice
Vibrate. It means to her she is there, inside.
The stammerer finds relief in speaking verses
Because it's less like talking. More like singing.

I mutter flakes of meaning. Foofaraw,
Shmagegeh. Blah-blah-blah.

A way of thinking a way of avoiding something.
Articulated grunts of grief and rage.
Even the *Iliad* yacks.

The baby rehearses melodies of speech,
The tunes of chat, of menace. Vocal
Without words, Morricone's music
Speaks for the iron faces of ugly cowboys.

Does her legendary "Yes, I can" exceed
*Requiem* itself? It is all one meaning. Now you
Really are saying something yes and can you?

Long before Stalin, long before everything,
The new lungs already learning to breathe,

Her tongue already studying its mission.

# In Flight

Speechifying Jaques shrugs his "As You Like It"
To persons from Duke to Clown, with Jaques himself

A player's word-flight made to seem as real
As Goya's astronauts in bird-bill headgear.

Intent and cool as bullfighters, they seduce
Us viewers to feel we too could fly, if only

We had those wings and hats. We learn to pronounce
The name as "Jayquis" not "Jacques," but courtly French

Enough, his second name might be Pierre.
The writer Jayquis-Pierre discloses his name

As Goya does his nature, *en modo de volar*—
This vapor of invention, lighter than air.

# Proverbs of Limbo

The Buddha is a liquor store
On a busy corner.

The proverbs of Limbo flutter
Between the flames of Righteousness
And the pits of Euphemism.

Gibberish and heredity. Runes
Of light, gnomons of shadow. Bromides
Of *of.*

The Committee on Narrative
Has condemned it, but nevertheless
It may be a lie.

*Listen*, begins a joke in the form
Of an aphorism, Cancer,
Shmancer—so long as
You have your health.

*Listen*. The author most quoted
In the Houses of Parliament
Is William Blake. Conviction
Resounds in the byways
Of bloviation. *"Amidst*
*The lustful fires he walks.*
*His feet become like brass."*

Clashes of theocracies.
The annals of begats and the orders of
Names both balance on the triple pillars
Of Identity of Mystery of Law, all bound
And refuted by the cardboard belt
God wears to amuse the angels.

# At the Sangoma

I asked the ancestors
About my suffering. You
Cannot understand it
You were born to
Too much of the possible.

If I was born free then what
Are you to me?
You were not born free,
To be born free, they said,
Would be not to be born.

I asked the ancestors
About their suffering.
Because it was ours, now
It is yours as the shape
Of your head is yours.

So I asked the ancestors
About the children. Is it

Their suffering too? That
Is your problem they said.
Honor it or not.

# Acknowledgments

I am grateful to the magazines in which many of these poems first appeared:

> *Agni Review, American Poetry Review, Blue Mountain Review, CNN Opinion, The New Republic, The New Yorker, The New York Review of Books, The New York Times Magazine, Plume, Salmagundi, This Broken Shore, Threepenny Review, The Washington Post Magazine, Yale Review.*

Several of the poems appear as lyrics on the PoemJazz album *Proverbs of Limbo*.

R.P.